Chemist

Field researchers

Scientists Ask Questions

By Ginger Garrett

Consultant
Linda Bullock
Science Curriculum Specialist

Children's Press®
A Division of Scholastic Inc.
New York   Toronto   London   Auckland   Sydney
Mexico City   New Delhi   Hong Kong
Danbury, Connecticut

Designer: Herman Adler Design
Photo Researcher: Caroline Anderson
The photo on the cover shows students conducting an experiment.

Library of Congress Cataloging-in-Publication Data

Garrett, Ginger, 1968-
  Scientists ask questions / by Ginger Garrett ; consultant, Linda Bullock.
    p. cm. — (Rookie read-about science)
  Includes index.
  ISBN 0-516-23614-8 (lib. bdg.)   0-516-24662-3 (pbk.)
  1. Science—Experiments—Juvenile literature. I. Title. II. Series.
  Q163.G295 2004
  507'.8—dc22
                          2004001224

CHILDREN'S PRESS, and ROOKIE READ-ABOUT®,
and associated logos are trademarks and or registered trademarks
of Scholastic Library Publishing. SCHOLASTIC and associated logos
are trademarks and or registered trademarks of Scholastic Inc.

12 13 R 13 12   62

What does a scientist do?

Archaeologists

A scientist asks questions.

Then a scientist experiments
to find answers.

Scientists use their eyes
and ears to experiment.

Scientists also touch and
smell to experiment.

Would you like to be a scientist today? First, you have to ask a question.

You might ask, "How can I get ketchup out of this plastic bottle?"

Next you must experiment.

Hold the bottle straight down. Does the ketchup come out?

If not, experiment again. This time, shake or squeeze the bottle.

Write down what you do.
Write down what happens.
You can also draw pictures.

Scientists write down what
they do. They also write
down what happens.

How did you get the ketchup out of the bottle? Did you find the best way?

Share your answer with someone else. Let them try to get the ketchup out the same way.

Scientists share their experiments. They tell others what they tried. They tell others what happened.

Scientists also share their answers. Sharing helps other scientists learn.

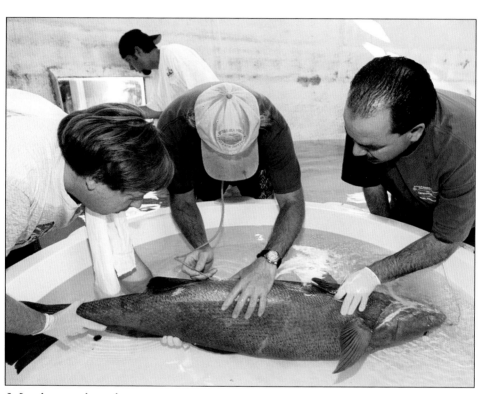

Marine scientists

Scientists use tools to experiment, too. Tools help scientists find answers. They use many kinds of tools.

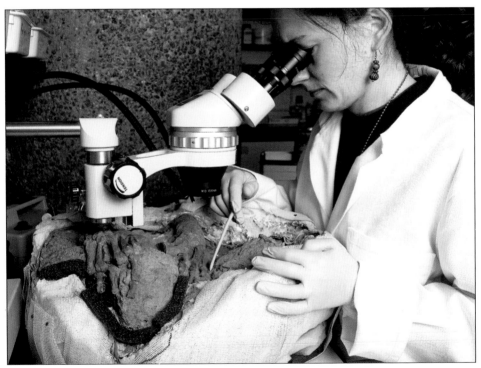

Archaeologist

A scale tells them how much something weighs. A microscope lets them see very small things.

Plant ecologist

A ruler is a tool. A ruler helps scientists measure.

A ruler measures how tall, or wide, or long something is.

Let's use a ruler to do another experiment.

How long is your pencil? Measure your pencil with a ruler.

Now measure a pencil that has never been used. Are both pencils the same length?

Think about why the pencils are different lengths. What did you learn from your experiment?

A pencil gets shorter as you use it. The shorter pencil has been used more often.

Scientists must think of the answers to their questions. Thinking is a scientist's job, too.

Researchers

Scientists ask questions.
They experiment to find
answers. They use tools.
They think.

How will you be a scientist
today?

Words You Know

bottle

experiment

pencil

ruler

scientists

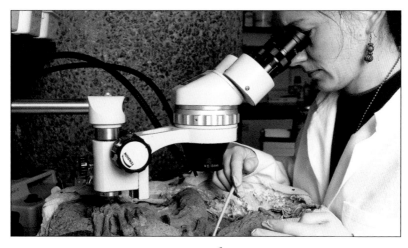
tool

Index

ears, 7

experiments, 4, 11, 16, 22, 25–26, 29

eyes, 7

ketchup bottle experiment, 8, 11, 15

measurements, 22, 25

microscopes, 19

notes, 12

pencil experiment, 22, 25–26

pictures, 12

questions, 4, 8, 29

rulers, 20–22

scales, 19

sharing, 15–16

smell, 7

thinking, 26, 29

tools, 18–22, 29

touch, 7

About the Author

Ginger Garrett is a writer who lives in Georgia. She has written articles for information technology products and a pharmaceutical company. She has introduced new drugs to doctors and educated medical staffs. She has also written a nonfiction book for adults on a medical topic.

Photo Credits

Photographs © 2004: Ellen B. Senisi: cover, 9, 10, 14, 23, 24, 30 bottom, 30 top left, 31 top left; Peter Arnold Inc./Roland Seitre: 21; The Image Works: 13 (Dick Blume/Syracuse Newspapers), 28 (Bob Daemmrich), 5, 30 top right (Philippe Gontier), 27 (Peter Hvizdak), 20 (Li-Hua Lan/Syracuse Newspapers), 6 (John Maier, Jr.), 18, 31 bottom (Museum of London/Topham-HIP), 3, 31 top right (Teake Zuidema); Visuals Unlimited: 17 (Richard Herrmann), 19 (Peter Lane Taylor).